To Think As a Pawn

(A Play in Three Acts)

by

Bill Peach

JM Productions
P.O. BOX 1911 • BRENTWOOD, TN 37024-1911

ISBN 0-939298-96-1

For information concerning additional copies, or permission
for dramatic production of the play, contact:

Bill Peach
400 Main Street
Franklin, Tennessee 37064
(615) 794-3855 or 794-6430

To Think As a Pawn, written by Bill Peach, involves a retired army officer's conflict with his 22-year-old son, a product of liberalism.

Major Ben Deutchman, as the stuffy officer Bruner, was both interesting and convincing, whether or not the audience agreed with the military philosophy that God approves of war and expects every man to do his duty for God and country.

Ray Curtis, as the son, held the attention of viewers as he presented his rebuttal over a chess game with his father whom he calls only "Colonel," a competent way to show total estrangement.

The short production came over strong in that it developed conflict, but made no attempts to answer the questions raised. Who can?

Sara Sprott Morrow
Nashville Banner
August, 1971

DEDICATION

The family in this book felt the impact of three wars, two from the past, and one yet to be fought. They exist in a world of fiction. Their voices convey oscillating trends on the subject of war, over a period of fifty-five years. The perceived credibility of each character rises and falls with the events of each day.

The first act was written during the Vietnam controversy; the second act was written as the Berlin Wall was being torn down; the third act is based on future events in Central America.

The final draft of this book was completed before the Iraqi invasion of Kuwait. This writer did not forsee the tragic events in the Middle East. There is no reference to Desert Storm. Only in a world of fiction can a family escape from the reality of war.

In the early 1940's, I sat in the lap of my grandmother and watched her tears dampen the pages of a World Atlas, tracing the uncertain steps of her son through Western Europe.

This book is dedicated to her, and to other, who have turned to another page and traced those steps through the sand of Desert Storm.

PREFACE

The first act of *To Think As a Pawn* was written for and performed by the Pulltight Players in August of 1971. The original cast included Ray Curtis, as Johnny Bruner; Carolyn Savage, as Mrs. Bruner; and the late Major Ben Deutchman, as Colonel Bruner.

As the mood of America changed, and the subject matter became less meaningful it lay dormant in a file drawer with other papers until the mid 1980's.

The suggestion for a sequel was brought to me by Cletus Sickler, writer for the *Nashville Tennessean.* From her idea, came Jeff Bruner, adding another generation to the saga of the Bruner family. After some thought, we saw some potential for even a trilogy. Hence, it logically became a three-act play.

The addition of Jennifer Bruner in the second act came from a suggestion from Dea Peach, who subsequently co-authored much of acts two and three. Through working with her on the play, the Bruner family and the Peach family developed a sensitivity and dialogue that neither family could have felt as deeply in 1971.

I am grateful for a lifetime of philosophical debate with the conservative and "pro-bellum" mood of Franklin, from which I tried to develop a valid and realistic philosophy for Colonel Bruner.

The character of Johnny Bruner evolved over two and a half decades. We grew together, from the radical defiance of the sixties, into a sense of maturity of adulthood in the mid nineties. We walked most of the roads together, with him always walking slightly to my left.

To Think As a Pawn is a study of confrontation and conciliation; conflicts of philosophy, age, gender, time, religion, patriotism, ethnicity, and intellect. It makes no attempt to find answers. It offers only questions.

It is a story of Kings, Queens, Knights, Bishops, and Pawns. Also, a story of sixty-four little squares, that make up one larger square. It is about what or where we are when the game begins. It is about who or why we are, when or if the game ends.

Bill Peach
February 19, 1991

Act I

CHARACTERS

Colonel John C. Bruner (Ret.), age 50
Mrs. (Clara) Bruner
Johnny Bruner, their son, age 22

May 1971

Colonel and Mrs. bruner are in the den of a recently decorated, Early American home. The decor reflects a mood of the Old South with a strong reverence for the past. A portrait of Colonel Bruner in uniform sits on a table. Other military artifacts are prominently displayed. Colonel Bruner is reading U.S. NEWS AND WORLD REPORT, *while Clara straightens some clutter from some of the furniture.*

COLONEL: Where's the boy?

CLARA: Upstairs in his room, I guess. He moved some things in about three o'clock. Just a few clothes and a lot of books. He hasn't been back downstairs since then. He hugged me, and kissed me, but he didn't have much to say. Have you spoken to him?

COLONEL: Not in the last four years. I haven't seen him. I don't know if I want to see him, or talk to him. I'm not sure I would recognize him. Does he look like all the other long-haired freaks? What's he gonna do? Does he have a job yet? Where's he gonna live?

CLARA: He looks fine. He's a little thinner than I
    expected, and of course four years older than I
    remember when he went off to school. Four years of
    college away from home can make a lot of difference.
    He's grown up, John.

COLONEL: Hell, at 22 it's time he grew up! He's old
    enough to be a man whether he acts like one or not.
    Damn, just think what he passed up! Any other kid
    would give his left arm for an appointment to West
    Point. "Cram it," he said. To me his father, he said
    that. I worked hard to get that for him. You don't get
    over something like that so easily in four years.

CLARA: I know you tried, John. You have to let him live
    his own life. He wasn't cut out to be like you. Be
    good to him, John. Be a father. Try to talk to him.
    We can do it.

COLONEL: About what? Maybe he's written some new
    poems. Do you think he brought us some flowers
    from the other flower children. How much do
    philosophy majors get paid a year? I don't even know
    who hires philosophy majors. Or was it liberal arts?
    I'm sure it was liberal. I don't know if they teach it as
    an art or a science.

CLARA: The newspaper story called it "University
    Studies." I don't know what that means. He seems
    very normal. He's just different. He does't think like
    you do. Why don't you go upstairs and talk to him?

COLONEL: Let's forget about him for a minute. I want
    to sit down with my wife and relax. I've had thirty
    hard years in the Army, and it feels good to retire.
    We're going to love this house. I like what you've
    done to it so far. There's a lot of tradition in this
    house. It's comfortable. This is a home for us, Clara,
    our first real home.

CLARA: All those places were home for me. It was just the moving around so much, and not ever knowing where you might be sent, or if you'd come back alive. I'm sorry the house isn't finished yet. I don't have the drapes for the master bedroom yet. I went shopping today. In fact, I went shopping every day this week.

COLONEL: I'm sorry you had to do all the work. I just couldn't leave until Tuesday morning. I spent all day Monday processing out. I went by to see Major McMillan at B Company. We were in Paris together in '45. We spent almost two hours re-living some old stories. We had some good times in Paris.

CLARA: Do you miss it, John?

COLONEL: I don't know yet. In a way I do. It will take some time. I saw a lot of places in thirty years. Most people never get the chance to travel most of Europe. The last few years back in the states were not very exciting. Mostly routine, and useless paper work. Anybody could have done that. You don't need combat trained colonels to sit behind a desk.

CLARA: I liked Fort Lee best of all. The buildings were nicer. I enjoyed going into Washington, and Mount Vernon, and seeing the Capitol and the museums. Do you remember the '53 inauguration? And the buttons that said "I like Ike?" Everybody liked Ike. I felt so happy for Mrs. Eisenhower that day. He was a first lieutenant when they married. She must have known all the time that he would be president someday. Their first child died as baby. Did you know that?

COLONEL: Yes, Ike was in the Infantry at Fort Sam Houston when they married. Their other son, what's his name, made lieutenant colonel before he retired.

CLARA: I always loved Mamie. There was something about her...a dignity, a charm.

COLONEL: *(Jokingly)* She was a Republican.

CLARA: *(Smiling, but sincere)* It didn't matter. She could have been a Democrat. If you're the wife of General Eisenhower. He was the right man for the presidency. He could've beaten anyone.

COLONEL: That was not a good year for intellectuals. Adlai Stevenson got less than 100 electoral votes. The man had no common sense. He couldn't speak the language of the people. He was all theory, and the people didn't know what he was trying to say. And Ike had a great war record. The '56 election was just as one-sided.

CLARA: Ike was something real. He was a good image for the country. People will vote for a man like that.

COLONEL: I wish I could have spent more time with you. I'll make it up to you now. You never once complained. We moved three times in one year, and I never heard one complaint from you.

CLARA: I could adjust. As long as we were together.

COLONEL: It was harder for the boy. Changing schools all the time. Maybe that's what's wrong with him. But he made excellent grades. Except that one year at the academy. Seventh grade, I think it was.

CLARA: He just wasn't happy there.

COLONEL: That year was good for him. They were strong on discipline. He needed a little of that. He hasn't been an easy kid to raise. I never could talk to

him. God, I wish he had gone to West Point! I
worked three years to get that appointment.

CLARA: You need to get out and meet some people.
Brother Anderson asked about you. He's at the Third
Avenue congregation. They built a new church out by
the shopping center. But I hear they're having some
trouble with some new young preacher.

COLONEL: Chaplain Walker is living here. I need to
look him up. I never did know what his religion was. I
don't think he's a Baptist, but I like him.

CLARA: Oh, I did ask about Jack Wolfson. He's not in
the store any more. He had a light stroke and his
nephew is running it.

COLONEL: Did you see anybody else we know?

CLARA: It's all new people. They tore down a whole
block between First and Second and built apartments.
I wish they would stop all this building. It was nice
the way it was. The traffic is terrible.

COLONEL: We're new people.

CLARA: You maybe. I grew up here. Six generations.
This was home to me until you carried me off to
Camp Shelby. Just tell them you live with me.
They'll accept you. Besides you're sort of a hero.
Which reminds me. Somebody, a Mr. Jackson. is
going to call you about speaking to the Lion's Club.
They meet at noon on Tuesdays. You might enjoy
that.

COLONEL: I think I'll visit around some before I join
anything. I need to get settled. I'm going to relax.
We have time to meet people. Let's plan to eat out a

lot and maybe see some movies. I drove by the theater. It looks funny.

CLARA: They spent a lot of money remodeling it. Some man from Nashville bought it. New seats and all and a wide screen. They showed two movies this week. And would you believe they were both rated R?

COLONEL: That's all they're showing now. I remember we used to go at least once a week. I just finally quit going. The language is terrible.

CLARA: Now remember, John. I heard some of your drill sargeants.

COLONEL: That's different. It's like what General Patton said in the movie. It's not offensive. Because that's the way people talk. I thought Scott did a great job. They didn't treat Patton fair in the script, but he played the character well. I could watch that over and over again.

CLARA: There's a DAR chapter here now. Mrs. Brighton called. She wants you for a speaker. You may need to hire me to be your agent. She's on the National Defense Committee and is in charge of programs.

COLONEL: I remember when her husband was killed. He was about 23 or 24. I think it was at Normandy. No, I'm wrong. It was in Belgium. The Martin kid is the one form here that died at Normandy. I remember reading about that. He had just made corporal.

CLARA: His wife never remarried.

COLONEL: That's a shame. She was so young. We've been lucky, Clara. God's been good to us.

CLARA: Johnny may go to work at the newspaper. He stopped by there on the way home, and he's going for an interview in the morning.

COLONEL: That's just what they need. A ninety year old conservative weekly paper, with Johnny Bruner, the liberal philosopher, to do their social events. Poetic spokesman for the radical left and part-time revolutionary. Byline, Johnny Bruner, "Mr. and Mrs. McGavock entertained guests at their bourgois mansion. Mrs. McGavock was attired in an elegant gown that cost enough to feed all the starving children in China." I can see that now. I hope they don't ever let him write editorials. Damn the country; damn the democracy; damn your parents! Make love in the streets! Legalize marijuana!

CLARA: Why don't you go up and see him? I remember when he was younger you two used to play chess at night. I loved to sit and watch. I unpacked your set and put it on the table. I thought it might be a way for you all to do something together.

COLONEL: I never had much luck teaching him the game. Maybe you could teach him to play bridge or hearts? Hell, chess is a man's game. I can't teach him anything. He's not going to listen to me, or talk to me. I don't think he'll stay here with us. I think he'll move out as soon as he can afford an apartment.

CLARA: He promised me he would try. You have to promise me the same thing. Give him a chance.

COLONEL: For what? It's been four years. I don't think he's gonna want to talk to me, about anything.

CLARA: Just be considerate. Try to understand his feelings. Don't provoke him. Don't mention Nixon or Agnew. Don't jump on him about West Point, and

don't fuss at him about ROTC. It wasn't compulsory.
He didn't have to take it.

COLONEL: It would have done him good!

CLARA: Just be a father. Let's be a family. You're fifty
years old. You're starting a new life. You've retired.
The military is behind you. You are a civilian now. I
think it will be different between you two, now. He is
your son, and he needs a a father.

COLONEL: I can't see it. I hope you're right. But he's
going to have to learn to show some respect if he
stays under this roof for long.

CLARA: And for God's sake please don't mention
Vietnam!

*(Johnny enters. He stops abruptly when he sees the
Colonel. His mood moves from fear, to caution, to
deliberation in that sequence.)*

JOHNNY: Hi, Mom. Welcome home, Colonel.

CLARA: I thought you had gone to bed. Could I fix you
something to eat?

JOHNNY: I just finished putting my things away. I
grabbed a sandwich on the way home, but thank you
anyway.

CLARA: I put clean sheets on for you. I had the movers
put everything as I remembered it when we lived
in...were at Fort Eustis. You were still a teen-ager
then. You may want some new furniture. I waited

about curtains. The others were so old I had to throw them away.

COLONEL: Why don't you fix us both some coffee, Clara? We might get out the chess board and try a game. I bet you didn't have time to play at school, reading all the time, and whatever else you did in your spare time.

JOHNNY: None for me, Mom, I've had enough today. One game. Just one and I gotta go to bed. I really haven't played in four years. Tell me if you get bored. I don't play very well.

(Mrs. Bruner exits for coffee. Colonel Bruner and Johnny set up the table and board. Johnny has the white pieces)

NOTE: Players should be familiar with the movements of each piece, and some basic strategy to give the appearance of an actual game. The Colonel's attitude is forceful and confident. Johnny is cautious and delaying.

JOHNNY: You tried to teach me as early as junior high. I remember you told me then, "Chess is really the history of the world in miniature. In 32 pieces of carved wood, you unfold it and re-live it."

(Mrs. Bruner returns with coffee for the Colonel and a glass of water for Johnny)

CLARA: Good night, all. I'm going to bed. Sleep late in the morning if you like. I'll fix breakfast when you get up.

JOHNNY: Good night, Mom. It's good to be back home.

COLONEL: We may be up late. See you in the morning.

JOHNNY: O.K., here we go Bobby Fischer and Boris Spassky. The great American champion and the Russian Commie.

(Moving a white Pawn to begin the match)

COLONEL: *(Ignoring the provocation)* You can measure the merit of man by the way he handles a chess match. His discipline, his courage, his leadership ability. It isn't like sitting behind a desk. This is out there where the action is. It takes strategy and daring. It's almost like being God. You control the destiny of Kings and Queens.

JOHNNY: This is all that's left, Colonel. Thirty years, three wars, and you command two ranks of tiny, wooden, toy soldiers. It's your move. Play it well.

COLONEL: My life hasn't been wasted. No matter what you think. I don't regret a minute of it. It hasn't been easy. I came back without a scratch, but I stumbled over more dead bodies than you can imagine. They made me sit out the last two wars, but I had some good years. I'm proud of what I did.

JOHNNY: Blood and guts Bruner. Stuck in the states and missed Korea and Vietnam.

COLONEL: There are some things you have to do whether you like it or not. If you love your country. If our nation survives. War is necessary. But they didn't teach you that at the university. Or did you have a war on campus? What did they call it? Was it a revolution? ls that what they called it? Did the National Guard massacre any innocent children where you were?

JOHNNY: No, I wasn't in the front lines. The National Guard was on campus two days. There was some rock throwing. Nobody got hurt.

COLONEL: The damn liberal professors cause it all. The kids are good, but the damn Communists run the schools. We'll have to fight them right here, sooner or later. The long haired hippie freaks will be marching with the Russians. Nothing is sacred to them. Burn it down! Blow it up! Maybe they should close the colleges. I don't understand what's going on. Why do we let it go on?

JOHNNY: We had this one teacher. He had taught political science for sixteen years. One day we were discussing Vietnam. He made some right-wing statement about Vietnam, and a girl called him a "Fascist." He threw a piece of chalk at her. They both apologized. We found out later that he was one of the prisoners rescued at Aushwitz. You can't always tell where everyone is standing in this confusing circle of life.

COLONEL: Kids nowadays have no respect for age, or tradition, or morality, or anything. It's a permissive age. I think it's just a small handful of radicals, and the others let them get by with it.

JOHNNY: Agnew says only 2% are militant and beyond help.

COLONEL: And they get all the attention. They think they know how to run the country. You never hear about the good kids who don't cause any trouble.

JOHNNY: That's the silent majority youth corps. Very
    happy. Very content with things as they are. They
    don't burn their draft cards. They don't run off to
    Canada. It's all very simple. If he doesn't say "no,"
    then you count him as a "yes" vote. Someone is jiving
    you, Colonel. You may have your numbers and your
    percentages reversed.

COLONEL: You play a good game of chess. You didn't
    forget everything I taught you. You're a little too
    cautious. You had good pursuit on my Queen, but
    you backed off. You should have used your Pawn to
    cover the King and attack with the Knight and Rook
    on on the Queen side.

JOHNNY: Good old pawns. Guard the left flank! Cover
    the right flank! Move straight ahead as far as you can
    and die. And God save the Queen!

COLONEL: Is anything real to you, Boy? Is it all really a
    joke to you? Can you laugh off 200 years of fighting
    and dying as some kind of game? Do you know why
    we didn't have to fight the Germans on American
    soil? You don't wait until they're at your front door.
    You don't crawl in a cave and hide. You take a stand
    somewhere. That's what we did. And the world is
    safe for democracy.

JOHNNY: That ended 26 years ago. You killed all the
    bad Nazi's. And the Japanese. The dirty, filthy,
    slant-eyes Japs. And you sat at your desk at Fort
    Gordon and held off the North Koreans. And now
    here comes Charley Cong! Crazy Communist Charley
    Cong! Why don't we let him have California with all
    the Hispanics and homosexuals and dig our trenches
    in Nevada somewhere?

COLONEL: I hope to hell you have a son someday. I
    hope this country survives long enough for you to
    have a son. I pity you. I sincerely pity you. Tell him

how it was before the Communists took over. Tell him what it was like to own property. Tell him about the times when we were allowed to vote, and to go to church, and to own your own business. Tell him how they took over without firing a shot. I hope he spits in your face!

JOHNNY: You don't see any other way? Your whole chronicle of history is written in blood. You don't see anything else in the future of mankind. A war for every generation. The eternal struggle between good and evil. Colonel, the struggle between good and evil is fought in other places. Not just on battlefields. And by people other than soldiers.

COLONEL: Did you ever study any history at all?

JOHNNY: Sure. But a lot of questions have never been answered. How long do you starve the civilians to feed the mercenaries? How much oppression can you impose before the people stand up and ask why? What do you do for diplomacy when you run out of marines? God be merciful on us when out great-grand-children look back at what we're doing in Vietnam!

COLONEL: The people of Vietnam have the God-given right to self-determination and freedom.

JOHNNY: Colonel, we financed the French military to keep the Viet Minh from winning independence. We refused to sign the Geneva agreement for a national election in 1956. And we appointed the first President of South Vietnam. In what way are we involved in self-determination and freedom?

COLONEL: You don't understand the Communists. You take your freedom for granted. People like you with no love for your country and no courage. You don't give a damn. You have your good life, and you don't care if the Communists take over the world as long as they don't bother you. You're parasites.

JOHNNY: Colonel, since 1945. Since World War II, you have been sitting behind a desk, in a soft job, funded by the taxpayer. Now you draw your retirement every month for the rest of your life. As long as you stay in the Army, all you have to do is lick some general's boots, and keep your butt covered, and fill out papers to make it look good. No thank you, Colonel. I'll take my lumps with the civilians.

COLONEL: Is that what you see me doing?

JOHNNY: How about the word "effete?" That's an Agnew word. It means you can't produce. You don't have to assume the responsibility of being a father, or husband, or compete in the real world.

COLONEL: Dammit, Boy, I was a soldier in the United States Army for thirty years. Doesn't that mean anything to you?

JOHNNY: Soldiers are sociological misfits. They live in a system with a different set of rules. It is unlike any other society. It isn't a democracy. It has a different standard of morality. It's a tyrannical, illogical pecking order based on rank, and rank has never been based on merit in the entire history of the military.

COLONEL: You have to have organization. You have to have leadership and discipline. You have to have some who are officers and others who are enlisted men.

JOHNNY: Enlisted men? Conscripted men? Drafted men? Outside the military it's called involuntary servitude. In most democratic societies it's considered un-constitutional.

COLONEL: Conscription is the right of the United States Congress to raise and maintain armies. And I would also have you understand that rank is based on merit. Look at men like Patton, and Eisenhower, and MacArthur.

JOHNNY: Careful on Eisenhower. He gave it up and became a politician. And warned us about the military-industrial complex. I'll concede to you on the other two. They were professionals. Warriors. Gladiators. Universal soldiers. They loved every minute of it.

COLONEL: And you laugh at that? What higher honor can a man achieve?

JOHNNY: Dying for your country. That's the highest honor a person can achieve. What more can you give?

COLONEL: Most men would die for their country. A lot of brave men have died for this country. You can't understand that. You can't think of yourself in that situation. It isn't all glory, and victory parades, and hugs and kisses when you come home. A lot of men didn't come home alive.

JOHNNY: I can see it in a telegram from the Department of Defense. "Dear Mrs. Bruner, we regret to inform you that your son is no longer in our employment. We mistook him for a Viet Cong, and hit him with friendly fire. Enclosed is a ribbon and medal to hang on your wall as a consolation for this most heroic service to his country."

(Colonel Bruner bounds angrily from his chair. He curbs an outburst, doesn't speak, then turns away from the table and walks away from Johnny. He stands with his back to Johnny. His face reflects anger, frustration, and sadness.)

Enter Mrs. Bruner

CLARA: Excuse me. I forgot my medicine. How's the
game going? Who's winning? Don't let me interrupt.
Go on and play. I'm going back to bed. It's so nice to
have my family back together again. I love seeing you
two together like this. Good night. See you both in
the morning.

*(Mrs. Bruner looks lovingly at her two men, very happy
and encouraged by the reconciliation she thought she saw.
Exit right.)*

JOHNNY: Has Mother been sick?

COLONEL: A little stomach trouble. The doctor says it's
just a nervous condition. She worries too much about
things. She's worried about you a lot these last four
years. Who's move is it?

(The Colonel sits down. He is calm.)

JOHNNY: Check! I just moved Queen to Queen Bishop
five. *(Pointing to board.)* You're butt's against the
wall!

COLONEL: *(After pondering his move)* That's no
problem. *(Colonel moves his King)* Thirty years ago,
the senators didn't run our wars. I just can't get used

to civilians making battlefield decisions. Back then, when the time came to fight, Congress declared war, and then left the fighting to the military. We fought to win.

JOHNNY: The times...they are a changing, Colonel. I read that somewhere, I think.

COLONEL: If we didn't have television and left-wing news media, this war could have been won a long time ago. We could have moved in and hit'em with everything we had, and it would have been over. A bunch of liberal senators kept it going for years with their conspiracy. That's what it is. We've never lost a war. We're not going to lose this one. It may take more men. It may involve invading North Vietnam, or even China. If it takes that, we'll do it.

JOHNNY: We? Who's we? You and me, Colonel?

COLONEL: The American people. And their backbone and courage. People who appreciate democracy and free elections, and self-government of the people.

JOHNNY: In Vietnam? Free elections in Vietnam?

COLONEL: Patriotism is not dead. Look around you, Boy! Look at the flags. They're everywhere. On car windows, in coat lapels, on top of buildings. Flags are flying in the yards of good God-fearing folks like us. Don't kid yourself, Boy. We're not all Communists, yet!

JOHNNY: How many things can you wear on one lapel? You've got a flag, a cross, a fish, a masonic pin, and some civic club pin. If somebody asks you what you believe, you just wave the lapel of your coat at them. You pour out you soul and your mind with a row of ornaments.

COLONEL: We love our flag! We are proud of it!

JOHNNY: But you have taken my flag away from me.
You use it to voice only your philosophy. If I walk
down the street carrying a flag, what do the people
passing by think? They would say, "Hey, there goes a
good kid. He's not one of those peace freaks. He
believes in the draft. He believes in killing those
gooks at My Lai." Pretty soon somebody's knocking
at my door to enlist me in the American Legion or
the Veterans of Foreign Wars.

COLONEL: Please discuss something seriously with me.
Can you do that? Can you be serious? A lot happened
in this world before you got here. You're 22 years
old, right? You don't have the privilege of being a
by-stander or on-looker. A lot of people went to a lot
of trouble to hold this world together until you got
here. You're probably going to be drafted. This is
not a choice. If your number comes up, you would be
drafted. Have you thought about that?

JOHNNY: Twenty-four hours a day, every day, for at least
four years. Yessir, I have thought about that.

COLONEL: You could burn your draft card, if you
haven't already.

JOHNNY: That doesn't make the problem go away.

COLONEL: You could run, to Canada maybe. I can see
you doing that. You don't look like one of those
hippies. But I believe I could see you doing
something like that.

JOHNNY: I can't see me doing that. I wouldn't run away.

COLONEL: So you would serve your country if you were
drafted. I know you're not going to volunteer. But if

you are drafted, you would put on your starched fatigues and pick up your rifle and be a good soldier?

JOHNNY: I can't see that, either. I don't know what I would have done in 1941. You heard the drum beating, and you followed your heroes to save America, and to fight for freedom. In the sixties, I heard a different drum, and followed my heroes for the same reasons. Your heroes died in France, in Belgium, and in Germany. Mine died in Dallas, in Memphis, in Mississippi, and at Kent State.

COLONEL: Not in Vietnam?

JOHNNY: They aren't asking to be heroes. They're asking for love, and understanding, and forgiveness. For me to forgive them for going, and for you to forgive them for not wanting to go, and for asking why they had to go.

COLONEL: At some time in your life, like it or not, you will have to face responsibility. You can't be a coward all your life. If I gave thirty years of my life for my country, surely you can give as little as two or three years in the military.

JOHNNY: Would you do five years in prison for your conntry?

COLONEL: Of course not! That's a dumb question!

JOHNNY: It isn't if it's one of your options.

COLONEL: You don't serve your country by going to jail. Do you want to be a criminal? What would people think?

JOHNNY: Then you wouldn't do five years in jail?

COLONEL: I wouldn't break the law. I respect and obey the laws of this land. So, I won't be going to jail.

JOHNNY: If you had been a German soldier in 1941, would you have pushed a Jew into the gas chamber at Auschwitz? If you had been a Russian soldier in 1956, would you have opened fire on the Hungarian students? If you had been a Roman soldier in AD 33, would you have obeyed orders and helped crucify Jesus Christ?

COLONEL: I was an American soldier! That's entirely different. Those are hypothetical questions. I wasn't in those kinds of situations.

JOHNNY: Would you have shot 102 women and children at My Lai?

COLONEL: That was one of the tragedies of war. That was a mistake. You don't always know who the enemy is. They may have been Viet Cong.

JOHNNY: A two year old Viet Cong?

COLONEL: I wouldn't have done it.

JOHNNY: What if you were ordered by your commanding officer to do it?

COLONEL: I wouldn't have killed an innocent child intentionally.

JOHNNY: Would you have dropped a bomb on a heavily populated city?

COLONEL: I wasn't a bomber pilot. I was in the infantry. I never had to make that decision. I don't know. I guess maybe I would.

JOHNNY: Would you refuse to obey an order of a commanding officer?

COLONEL: When you're in a war, you have to obey orders. If you don't, you cause a lot of problems. If you foul up some mission, or refuse an order. You follow the rules. You do what you're ordered to do. You have no choice.

JOHNNY: Then you would do it?

COLONEL: I would conduct myself as an American soldier. That's what I did for thirty years. I'm not ashamed of that. I believe in the military code. I feel good about my record as a soldier.

JOHNNY: How do you feel about your record as a human being?

COLONEL: I care about people. That's why I enlisted and served my country. I was a soldier because I do have feelings. Being a soldier was my responsibility as a human being.

JOHNNY: You don't see any conflict at all? Between the moral code of the military, and basic human rights? Does military justice fit anywhere into everything that we all believe about the sanctity of life and all the laws we've written to protect the rights of all humankind?

COLONEL: Damn it, Boy! War is hell. You don't have time or the choice to call a civil liberties lawyer, or appeal to a a judge, or to look up some Bible verse to find out what you should do every time. You do what you have to do. To hell with civil law! In times of crisis we have martial law.

JOHNNY: For how long?

COLONEL: As long as the crisis exists!

JOHNNY: Cold war? Pre-war? Undeclared war? Or post-war crises? Is the absence of war, just an interruption to a continual war? You veterans measure time from the end of the last war. Is peace just a period of nothingness in the military history of civilization? If you are a Civil War buff, you live in the year 106. If you fought in World War II then you see this as the year 26. What ever happened to BC and AD?

COLONEL: Wars are not popular. Most people, like you, are are only concerned with their own freedom. And they don't care about the little countries and the helpless people of the world. You can't see or understand it. The civilian mind can't grasp this. You have to depend on the military to know what's going on in the world. The people just can't understand the dangers. The War of 1812 wasn't popular. Everybody loved the War of Independance. But without the War of 1812, we would be British colonies. Are you going to let the Nazi's, or the Communists take over the little countries of the world?

(As the colonel is speaking, Johnny studies the Colonel's previous move. He realizes that the game is over. He cannot move to avoid losing. He calls this to the Colonel's attention.)

JOHNNY: Checkmate! You've won Colonel!

COLONEL: *(Not looking at the board)* Hitler would have marched across Europe and would have taken Russia. England would have been bombed into oblivion. He took most of France. Hitler took over all the little countries of Eastern Europe. Do you know what the

world would be like today if we hadn't invaded
Germany?

*(The Colonel rises from his chair, and is almost screaming
at Johnny, hearing nothing that is being said.)*

JOHNNY: The game, Colonel! You've won the game.

*(The Colonel is still standing. Ranting. completely out of
touch with the chess game.)*

COLONEL: You're goddamn right we won! Thank God
that three hundred thousand young American
soldiers were willing to die. Twelve million took up
arms and stopped that syphillitic madman. You're
damn right we won! You don't think too much of that.
You have no idea what war is like. You don't know
what it is to risk your life for freedom. You fight wars
to win. You don't lose wars! Winning is all that
counts. Survival! We're free! Goddammit boy, why
can't you see that. We destroyed that maniac and his
Nazi whore, and the storm troopers and the Gestapo.
We hanged twelve of them after Nuremberg!
Himmler, Georing, Hess, Eichmann! If they didn't
commit suicide, we got 'em. We got 'em all!

JOHNNY: The game is over. I can't move. You've won,
Colonel.

(The Colonel regains his composure. stops his oration. sits down. The two look at each other with uncertainty. there is a lengthy silence.)

JOHNNY: That was a great move. I couldn't move anywhere. You are just too good for me.

COLONEL: Set'em up again, Boy. One more game before bedtime. You almost had a me couple of times. We have time for one more game. It's just ten-thirty. I'm not very sleepy. Chess keeps we wide awake. I could play all night.

(The Colonel carefully begins placing his pieces in the proper positions on the board. Johnny does not. He does not touch his pieces. He sits back in his chair and watches the Colonel. He does not speak.)

(The Colonel begins speaking very calmly and with measured deliberation, choosing his words very carefully.)

COLONEL: Peace is a dream, boy. We all want peace. But peace is not something you just wish for or pray for. You fight for peace. But you can't remain free very long without military power. We're now at a time in history when we have no other choice but to fight. We can't be like we were before World War II. We can't afford to be isolationists. We've become the greatest power on earth, whether we want to be or not. Set 'em up. One more game. We can't deny this awesome responsibility. Innocent people are being killed every day by the filthy Communist dictators. America never starts a war. We will never start a war. We only go to war when we have to. Wars begin long before the first shot is ever fired. We may look back at today and see it as an early part of

World War III. We've been able to avoid another world war, because of our nuclear power. They're afraid of us. We probably should have gone on and fought China all-out instead of ending in a stalemate in Korea and Vietnam. Set 'em up. One more game. Your game has improved. Set 'em up. Let's play one more. Just one more game.

JOHNNY: No more, Colonel. You're too good for me. I'll never be able to beat the grand chess-master.

COLONEL: Courage, Boy! Don't quit with one defeat. Where's your spirit? You don't love this game like I do. I could play all night. I love the risk, the danger, the game strategy. The struggle for victory, the daring moves.

JOHNNY: Okay, one more. Then I have to go to bed. Have your fun while you're winning.

(Johnny now leans forward and begins to place his pieces on the board. The Colonel smiles, rubs his palms together, and gets ready for another game.)

COLONEL: This country is losing its war-like spirit. There is no great patriotic fervor anymore. We are in the beginning of a great decline in America. We may go the way of Rome. We need to do something to wake up the great American spirit. We need to motivate the courageous American men and women of yesterday. Great nations are built getting ready for and fighting wars. In peacetime, people forget and become lazy and complacent. We've got to renew the energy of the American people.

(Johnny has placed all his pieces on the board, except one of his pawns. He leaves it sitting off the board, on the table, toward the audience. The Colonel continues not having detected the error.)

War's just another part of national policy. It's just one more function of government. The Constitution gives Congress that power. When diplomacy and debate break down, it's the last resort. But, you have to be prepared all the time. You have to be ready. *(The Colonel points to the missing Pawn.)* You left off one Pawn. We have to maintain a standing army. We must have skilled, well- trained fighting men. *(Pointing to Pawn again.)* You left off one Pawn. Come on let's play. One more time. Here we go. Let's do it. War is part of God's plan. The Old Testament is a chronicle of the struggle of God's people. David, Samson and Joshua. War is cruel, but it's better than slavery. It's better than being in bondage. Defeat is far more cruel than any act of war could ever be. *(Pointing to Pawn)* You left off one Pawn. Are you going to play or not? War's have to have the support of all the people. Once war is declared, it's a national effort. It unites the common feelings of all the people. It gives us a sense of duty, a sense of purpose, an humble feeling, a willingness to sacrifice yourself for something greater in life. Something more important than your own limited struggles. You get caught up in the excitement of battle. Let's play. Your move. Set up your other Pawn and move.

JOHNNY: It doesn't want to play!

COLONEL: That's funny. Set it up. Give me your best opening shot.

JOHNNY: It doesn't want to play. That Pawn doesn't
   want to play anymore. It's tired of playing chess.
   Chess is no fun to a Pawn.

COLONEL: Now you're being silly. Are you giving me a
   handicap? This is chess, Boy. It isn't horse racing or
   bowling. Everybody has the same chance to win.
   Your move.

JOHNNY: Have you ever thought just what it's like to be
   a Pawn in a chess game? It just moves forward. To
   capture or be captured. It has no value unless it just
   happens to be in the right place to protect another
   piece. You don't cry over the loss of one Pawn. You
   sacrifice the pawns to capture knights and rooks. As
   long as you save the King. What are pawns? It
   doesn't matter if you lose sixty thousand or a million
   pawns, as long as the game is not lost. Even a Pawn
   should have some right of choice in the destiny of its
   own life.

COLONEL: Okay, you've made your point. Now let's
   play. So, you're the pawn? Then who am I? The
   Knight, the warrior who rides into villages and
   frightens the people. Am I the Queen? Surely you're
   not saying I'm the Queen. Then I'm the King. I must
   be the King. A helpless, useless King surrounded and
   protected by you and the other pawns.

*(Johnny begins speaking cautiously and builds to an
emotional rage.)*

JOHNNY: No, you're not the King. You're an unpayable
   debt of endless causes, noble motives, and obsolete
   weapons...

You're several thousand years of rules and
regulations, of passions and misconceptions. You are
one of thirty million in this country who wear the rank
of veteran...

You control the lives and dominate the thinking of all
of us. You're a link in an unbroken chain of eye for
eye, tooth for tooth, orphans for orphans, widows for
widows...

You spent your life grooming for war. If we didn't
have a war you would have to find one somewhere
else. Peace just leaves you out in the cold...

War is a testing ground for generals and colonels. A
reason for people like you to exist. You have to
create all kinds of false alarms, you rekindle old
prejudices, and you bring us to the brink of war and
then you come riding in on a white horse to save us...

When war comes, you are the self-created champion
of the people. And it's all under the banner of peace...

Colonel, you've lived into a time in which there are
no more military heroes. An age of impersonal
technology. We're button pushers, missle launchers,
and bomb droppers. We are anonymous, non-heroic,
destroyers of cities...

We don't give medals anymore for bravery. We give
medals for losing an eye, or a leg, or an arm, or your
life. There are no more healthy, complete, living
heroes. We all lose. There are no winners.

The ones who really pay the price. The nineteen and
the twenty year olds. The black kids, and the poor
white kids. Can you hear they crying in the streets?
They're saying, "Hell no!" They know what you've

been doing to them for all these years. They don't believe you anymore...

You are the match-makers, the promoters, just the public relations men for the next performance...

You sit with Spiro Agnew in the top row of the upper deck and laugh at the cacaphony of the student protests. Your ears have been trained to hear only the drums, the bugles, and the trumpets. Every sound you hear is a call to war. If you could sit with us down front, on the front row, you could hear the strings and the woodwinds...

You talk about freedom and self-determination. Tell me about Vietnam and self-government. Explain the rules of the Geneva Convention to me. Play the game all the way, Colonel. Help me understand the rules.

You have to see the brutality and the stupidity of it all. You have to know it's wrong. Don't tell me that killing is beautiful, or humane, or patriotic if it is done by someone in uniform. Am I to grow up to be one of another generation of savages? Some tribal warrior? Colonel, you have the misfortune of having sired a misfit.

If there is one thing that I ask; if there is one thing that I demand of myself; it is the moral courage not to play the game. Like a lot of other young men in the world, I will not kill another human being, or be killed without knowing what I am killing or dying for.

You may have seen your last generation of warriors. One day, long after you and I have gone, the young men of the world will see the emptyness of military heroics. They will stop listening to your glittering portraits of blind patriotism, and see what it all really is. When you take off the uniforms, and the medals, and the ribbons. When they quit beating the drums, and blowing the bugles. When the tribal chanting has stopped. When you rip the mask off of the gallantry of dying and you expose the infamy of killing. When the crowd stops cheering and the band stops playing...

When everything is quiet you can see and hear what it really is...the naked, criminal brutality of mass murder. It's not a game anymore.

You're a good chess player. Chess will never change. You have no problem there. But, war has changed. That's your problem. It's good to have you back home, Colonel. I'll see you in the morning. Good night.

(Johnny turns and exits toward stairway.)

The Colonel stares at the board. He picks up the one Pawn sitting off the board. He looks at it, hesitates, holds it in his hand, clutches it, and finally carefully places it in its proper position on the board. He stares at the board, then with one sweep of his hand, in disgust, knocks over all the white pieces, scattering them on the table and on the floor.

Curtain

ACT II

(September 1990)
John (Johnny) Bruner, age 41
Jeff Bruner, Son, age 17
Jennifer (Jenny) Bruner, Daughter, age 15

Narrator:

*The family has returned from the cemetary and the burial
of Colonel John Bruner, who died day before yesterday at
his home of an apparent heart attack. Colonel Bruner's
wife had died in the mid-seventies and Johnny, his wife
and two small children had come to live with the Colonel.*

¤   ¤   ¤

*As the second act opens, Johnny and Jeff are sitting at a
table on which a chess board is sitting. The chess pieces
are at random positions indicating an unfinished game,
but the two are not playing. They are just sitting, looking
at the floor, very pensive, not speaking. Jennifer is sitting
on a couch across the room, holding a book, but not
reading, wiping her eyes occasionally and quietly crying.*

JOHN: I was so glad that Chaplain Walker did the eulogy.
He and the Colonel had been so close since they
retired. They had coffee together almost every
morning at Clara's. It was his only link with the
military. As long as the two of them were together,

he could still sort of stay in touch with the past. They spoke the same language.

JEFF: I was surprised that you would have a military funeral. Those guys in the color guard were so sharp. Every movement was just in perfect timing.

JOHN: It's what he would have wanted.

JEFF: But, knowing how you feel. I thought, you know what I mean.

JOHN: It was his funeral. What I feel doesn't matter. I would have done anything for him. When we moved here, after Mom died, you and Jennifer were just babies. I was working late at the paper every night. He was so good to your mother, and loved you so much. You were his joy. You were the son to him that I never was. You gave him a new life. He was young again. It was as if he had a second chance to have a family.

JEFF: I know. He told me that. Not in just those exact words. But I felt it. He kept talking about... not really talking about...just mentioning those years. I can't believe what you did to him. If I could have had the opportunities that he made for you. What you did was a slap in the face.

JOHN: But he understood. Much later. But he understood.

JEFF: But you know he was hurt.

JOHN: He was dissappointed, and frustrated. He failed at something. He could do anything. He was a commander. And I was a source of frustration. I was his only failure.

JEFF: You could have made it at West Point. He told me that you made maybe one "B" in high school and were valedictorian or something and then after that you didn't try. You finished college, sure, but a state university with no preparation for a career.

JOHN: Jeff, I am the editor and publisher of this town's only newspaper. I have a career. I have a job. I get up every morning and go to work and make a living. I make a little money, I have fun, and on some occasions I even think it might make a difference in the world. Maybe not the world. Maybe I touch just a few people. If not, at least it makes me feel better.

JEFF: But you could gone to West Point. Think what that would look like, on a diploma hanging on your wall. You could get a job anywhere. Doors would open for you. Think of what it would have meant.

JOHN: When you graduate from West Point, you have a job. You sign away your soul, and your mind, and your individual being. I don't want that kind of job. I didn't then and I don't now.

JENNY: Right on, Jeffie! *(Singing)* Be all that you can be. Join the Army. *(Oratorical)* Travel to exotic, distant lands. Meet exciting, unusual people and kill them...

JEFF: Shut up! I have looked at that dumb poster until I could puke. Why don't you haul your pre-teen emotional problems up to your room and lock yourself in.

JOHN: Jennifer, this may need to be some quiet time between Jeff and me. We both have a big void to fill.

JENNY: I'm OK. I'm reading. I just thought that was kinda funny. Why would somebody with a three digit IQ want to go to West Point? Would you major in **brain bashing? Maybe with a minor in throat slitting?**

Hey, get a BA. What's that? A BA? That's a degree in barbaric arts.

JEFF: That nerd is going to get it if she says one more word to me.

JENNY: Dad, see if he's armed. I think he may have a government issue M-16 rifle under his coat.

JOHN: Jennifer, ease off. This is not the time for bitchy dialogue.

JENNY: Lock and load one clip! Commence firing! Check the body count.

JOHN: If you insist on ridicule as your only mechanism of debate then you don't need to be in this conversation.

JEFF: Right on dad! *(Turning around)* Come back from that now. I'm tired of your big mouth, and your childish jokes. You want a body count? We can add one more!

JENNY: Dead! One hostile female caucasian of undetermined political attachment, suspected Communist. Score one for the young soldier. And his articulate apologist! *(Exit)*

JOHN: Jennifer Bruner! Come back here! *(She returns)* *(Calmly, with sarcasm)* I have no argument with your philosophy, or your skills with the language, but until you develop some compassion and civility, you are not pleasant company. *(Exit Jenny)*

JEFF: You two make a great comedy team. The flower child and the draft dodger. You would have been right at home in the sixties.

JOHN: I was very much a part of the sixties, but I was not a draft dodger. I was a draft evader. There is a fine line of difference. I did six years in the Reserves.

JEFF: Do you call that patriotism? Is that service to your country? Did they give you some kind of medal for that? Do you just overflow with pride for that?

JOHN: I was patriotic two Thursday nights and one Sunday every month for six years. I put on my freshly starched fatigues, drove to Nashville, pounded on a typewriter, filled out some papers. I let them believe I was a soldier for a few hours and came home and went back to work the next morning. And all those things that you ask me to die for...freedom, religion, family, morality, free enterprise, self-determination...I gave up three times a month, and two weeks every summer. The military didn't give me those things. It took them away from me. I believe in those values. What do you think I do six days a week? I serve my country, when I write something defending these values. All those things, all those things that I love, do not exist in the military. It was the military that took away my freedom, my religion, my morality, my self-esteem.

JEFF: When you had Sunday drills, did you have a break for church service? Or did you have any religion back in sixties? Did you go to church then?

JOHN: There was a chaplain in the unit and they had some kind of assembly. It was a generic inter-faith philosphy of saluting God and generals that I never understood. For a while they let four of us sort of slip away to a church over on West End Avenue, but we had on our fatigues. I had some guilt feelings inside a church. I know God is everywhere, but a church building is officially his turf and I felt out of place wearing a costume that defied the very essence of Christianity.

JEFF: You really hated the military. That's obvious. You don't like it, so everybody else should hate it. I read your editorial on high school ROTC. But you couldn't stop it. We got it. I know you don't talk to me, but I know what you think. I read your editorials. If kids ask me what my dad is like I tell them to read page two. This is my dad. That's how much I know about him. I know he doesn't like the National Rifle Association, the Contras, Civil War re-enactments, military monuments, and war toys.

(Jenny enters, passing through)

JENNY: I need a drink of water. You left out *(Enumerating)* Dan Quayle, Jimmy Swaggart, live studio wrestling, deer hunting, capital punishment, Nazis, skinheads, and the Klan. If you're gonna keep pace with the Bruner mentality, you're gonna have to read the paper on a more regular schedule, Little Brother! *(Exit crossing)*

JEFF: You have the newspaper and everybody reads it but you've lost your credibility by always being against something. Every week there is something else that you don't like. You condemn everybody for what they do and what they believe, but you don't do anything. People see you as a wimp. Just one time, why can't you be for something instead of against it? I don't understand what's in your mind. Why are you so bitter?

JOHN: Would you feel better if I had killed a Vietnamese?

JEFF: That's some kind of dumb question! Of course not!

JOHN: Would you feel better if a Vietnamese had killed me?

JEFF: Dad, I love you and I'm glad you're alive. And I don't want to hear that kind of crap from you. You aren't writing an editorial. You're talking to your son who just watched some men pitch dirt on his grand-father's casket. I don't need to discuss dying. This has not been one of the best days of my life.

JOHN: Jeff, I'm sorry. You deserve a better father than I have been.

JEFF: No. Let's don't do the guilt trip. Just tell me you love me, and want what's best for me, and you will try to do better in the future. That's all I need.

JOHN: I'm serious. It's my fault. I do love you. I'm glad you spent so much time with the Colonel. Your relationship with him was so good for both of you. I could see the love between you two. I can't replace him. I can't be what he was to you. That can't be replaced.

(Long pensive pause. Both grope for the next line.)

JEFF: While we're sitting here talking, there is something I need to tell you. I had been afraid to tell you. I thought you would just ingore me and walk away, so I just couldn't tell you. Eventually, I would have told you. I was afraid to ask you. I did tell Mom, but I just didn't know how to tell you.

JOHN: About ROTC?

JEFF: Jennifer told you?

(Jennifer enters from kitchen with glass of water)

JENNY: I did not! I didn't tell anybody because I didn't
    believe it myself. I know some of the freaks who take
    ROTC and my brother, dumb as he is, wouldn't be
    one of those. I didn't tell anybody. And I would
    rather nobody ever knew. And don't you ever offer
    me a ride home after school on days you wear your
    uniform. I will walk home. In the rain, in the snow, in
    the mud. But I am not going to be seen with some
    punk high-school play soldier.

JOHN: Jennifer! Go...to...bed! Now! This very minute!

(She runs, spilling water, wipes it up with her hand)

JEFF: You taught her well. That's your baby daughter,
    Dad. She is her father's child. Like father, like
    daughter.

JOHN: My arms aren't long enough to hug you both at the
    same time. You have to realize that much of what
    she thinks and says, and does is because of you. She
    reaches around you to touch me, just like you and the
    Colonel reached around me to touch each other.

JENNY: *(Reappearing at exit left.)* Did you hear that, Jeff
    Bruner? You have created a monster. If there
    weren't people like you, we wouldn't need people
    like me.

(Jennifer disappears before anyone can respond.)

JOHN: I'm sorry. You asked how I knew about ROTC. Sargeant Hargrove called and told me. Really, he sort of asked me if it was all right. It was after you had signed up, or enlisted, or whatever you do. He knew it was awkward for all three of us. I'm sure he read my editorial.

JEFF: Why would he call you?

JOHN: He wanted to see how I felt about it and he wanted to eliminate some concerns that I might have about what he might be teaching.

JEFF: How do you feel about it? Is it OK? If I had asked before I signed up, would you have told me I couldn't?

JOHN: I didn't take ROTC in college. It was compulsory my freshman and sophomore years, but I found a legal way out of it. How do I feel about it? You read my editorial. Would I have told you not to? No. If I told you couldn't, you would have wished for the rest of your life that I had let you. But if you do, then you have the rest of your life to wonder why you did.

(Jennifer enters right, dressed for bed. Crosses backstage toward exit left)

JENNY: The rest of your life. Second lieutenants live to be twenty-one. They lift them up on a long pole to see where the sniper fire is coming from. *(Exit left)* *(From off-stage Jennifer is singing.)* Where have all the

flowers gone? Long time passing. Where have all the
flowers gone? Long time ago...

JOHN: He had some questions to ask me. In an editorial,
I had written something to the effect that ROTC
should teach you how to napalm babies, burn huts,
rape Vietmanese women, and shoot hogs and cows.
He just wanted to assure me that those were not his
intentions, and were not included in the curriculum,
at least not at high school level.

JENNY: *(Enters left singing)* Gone to graveyards everyone.
When will they ever learn? When will they ever
learn? *(Exits right.)*

JEFF: It's not like that. You don't understand. It's things
like camping, and parade drill, and first aid and just
learning to be a better citizen.

(From right, Jennifer falls onto stage floor as if dead.)

JENNY: Oh! *(Clutching her chest)* Bring me a band-aid!
I've been hit by a mega-millimeter, full metal jacket,
heat seeking nuclear device. Where is the good
citizen with the band-aid. Help me! Private Bruner!
I'm bleeding! Hurry! Bring me a band-aid!

JEFF: Please make her leave the room, before I hit her.

JENNY: ROTC if for geeks and little boys who are too
old to be boy scouts and too young to be Marines, and
too dumb not to know the difference. *(She gets up)*

JOHN: Jennifer, I am trying to talk to Jeff. Shhh! Stop it!

JOHN: *(Back to Jeff)* The sargeant was explaining what the ROTC curriculum included. He listed several things. I forgot what all he said. Then he said that they taught oral communication. I broke up on the phone. I thought about all the drill sergeants I had known. Did they just miss that class completely? I suggested to him that maybe that could be taught better in the English or speech department.

JENNY: *(Goes to kitchen, marching in cadence)* Lay-uf, lay-uf, leff, rite, leff, hupp, do, re, fo, yo leff, yo leff, yo leff, rite, leff...*(Returns from kitchen)*

JOHN: Young lady, I'm telling you again! I am getting tired of your interruptions, and your disrespect for your brother. I have told you twice to go to bed. We have had a rough day and have a busy day tomorrow. None of us need to be up at midnight playing vicious games with each other.

JENNY: Daddy, it's only eleven. I can't go to sleep. *(Goes toward exit right and turns.)* I'm sorry. For our young recruit, the time is now 2300 hours. *(Turns toward exit, and turns back again.)* And for all you marines, wherever you are, Mickey's long arm is pointing to twelve, and his short arm is pointing to eleven.

(John rises, goes toward right. Jennifer runs. John turns and walks back toward table. Jeff looks toward exit right. While John's back is turned, Jennifer re-appears at right and gives Jeff a snappy military salute followed by a left hand on right bicep with raised clenched fist gesture.)

JEFF: She has no feeling for anything. She was so mean to the Colonel. He tried to love her. They were a lot like you and him. Not that you were mean to him, but just that you never understood him.

JOHN: I share your respect for him. He was a good man.
When you and I talk about him, we call him the
Colonel. There was never anything disrespectful
about calling him that. He was a symbol. It meant
one thing to me and something else to you, and to
him it was even something else. He put on a uniform
and went to work every morning, and he worked hard
at being a colonel.

(Shift in mood to pensive and broken narrative)

The fact that I don't understand why, and the fact that
I don't hold that job in high esteem, did not diminish
my love for that man. It was a role that he felt some
compulsion to play. When he wasn't working, when
he wasn't being a Colonel, he was a gentle and kind
and loving man. It took me a long time to learn that.
When I was in my late teens, I lost him. He was away
and Mom and I were alone. He lived only in my
impressions of all the colonels and generals in the
world. I saw an unending war between the military
and the civilians, and we were on opposing sides. I
loved him very much twice in my life. Once when I
very young, and once when he was very old. Those
years in between, I miss very much.

JEFF: We talked about it. Sometimes he would be telling
me a story about something he did or saw in Germany
or somewhere, and he would say, "I don't think I ever
told Johnny about that." I knew why. I understood.

JOHN: There are some things in his room that he would
want you to have. He kept his uniforms. He never
put them on because he knew they wouldn't fit
anymore. About once a year, I would drop some moth
balls in the pockets. They just hung in the closet.

JEFF: Do you not want them? They are legally yours by right of inheritance. You have first choice.

JOHN: Don't make jokes about that.

JEFF: But you don't have any uniforms, and I have mine for ROTC. You shoud have at least one set of dress greens.

JOHN: That isn't funny.

JEFF: He saw you. He watched you from his upstairs bedroom. He cried when he told me. The only times I ever saw the Colonel cry was when he talked about Grandma, and when he told me about watching you burn your uniforms. You piled them on a garbage can lid, and burned them.

JOHN: I didn't have to wear them anymore. Six years was enough. I didn't realize he watched. It was a private thing I had to do for myself. It was a personal ritual. I am sorry he saw it. I thought I had waited until everyone was asleep.

JEFF: He told me you burned your draft card.

JOHN: Not really. I burned three draft cards. But they were all obsolete. Every time my classification changed I took the old card and burned it. It was all legal. It just felt good. It never was illegal to burn a draft card. Most people didn't understand that. It was a gesture. The law said you had to have your classification card in your possession at all times. If you burned your draft card and you then didn't have one, that's when you broke the law.

JEFF: So you really didn't break the law? It was just a gesture of protest?

JOHN: Yes I did. From the day I was 18 until my last day in the Reserves, when I was 28, I never ever carried it on me. I knew where it was, but I never carried it. I technically violated a federal law for ten years.

JEFF: You've got some serious hang-ups with the military!

JOHN: Seriously, when you feel like it. Go through his things and take whatever you want. Later, when we both feel better we can pack the rest in the attic or somewhere.

JEFF: You don't care about anything that was his. You don't want anything that was his. That's cold and that's cruel.

JOHN: I loved him! It would not be fair to him for me to have what to me are trinkets of vanity. Things that to him were his life.

JEFF: Trinkets of vanity!

JOHN: They mean nothing to me apart from him. I feel what they meant to him. I never loved what he was. I loved him.

JEFF: He told me a lot of things. He told me about your first night home after you finished college. He tried to teach you to play chess.

JOHN: I knew how to play chess. He just wanted to be sure that he could still beat me.

JEFF: You won't play a game you can't win. Chess was his game. You never liked it because he could always beat you.

JOHN: I tried to play chess with him. No, I really didn't. I never gave him a second chance after that first night.

It was never mentioned again. I used to watch him
sometimes. He would unpack the pieces and set up
the board and move a few pieces. But, I don't think
he ever played until... You were probably in the first
grade. You asked why the Queen could move
anywhere she wanted to, and thought it was funny
that only Knights could jump over something.

JEFF: We had some good times. There was one game
that lasted almost a month. I would come in from
baseball practice, make a few moves, and we would
leave the board, and after I had showered and done
my homework I would go in to finish the game, and
he would be asleep. In the chair in front of the board.
Just snoring away.

JOHN: Maybe you can help me improve my game.

JEFF Do you want to finish this game? *(Pointing to board)*

JOHN: No, not his game. We can start another one, if you
like.

JEFF: I almost had him in check. He started to move a
piece. And then he leaned back. He looked strange.
It wasn't as if he were deciding what to do. He leaned
forward and moved a piece that no meaning. It was
like me when I was six years old, just moving a piece
to some space that was open. And then he leaned
back in the chair. There was a grimace on his face. I
guess some pain. No sound. Just a brief grimace of
pain.

JOHN: That's when you ran upstairs to get me?

JEFF: I knew he was dying. The look on his face was not
so much that he was dying, but that he couldn't finish.
The thing that he was doing, he couldn't finish. It
wasn't life, it was the next moment in life that he
wanted.

JOHN: Sometimes you amaze me. There is so much feeling and understanding inside of you. How have I missed that?

JEFF: Do you want to finish the game for him?

JOHN: What if I lose it for him?

JEFF: Losing is your problem. You have to deal with that.

JOHN: Did you ever beat the Colonel?

JEFF: Not once! Never! Sometimes I would think I was going to beat him. I could always tell he knew that I didn't have a chance. And I guess now I am glad I never did.

JOHN: You would derive some satisfaction from beating me?

JEFF: Sure.

JOHN: I don't want to finish his game. I would feel like some relief pitcher coming in with two out in the bottom of the ninth.

JEFF: Sorry, you don't have that option. Who do you think you are? Are you Adam? Do you think everything that has ever happened just goes away and you start all over? No way! You have to finish his game for him because he can't. He's not here anymore, and you're his only son.

JOHN: What's this sudden intimidation? You say I intimidate you. Who's dictating whose life? Give me some space!

JEFF: If your sweet little Jenny wants to abolish apartheid, or trash a pro-life rally, or be a Unitarian missionary to Armenia, all I hear is applause. All I ask from you is approval, and all I hear is ridicule. What did I hear you ask her? Is ridicule your only mechanism of debate? That's all I ever hear from you.

JOHN: Approval? Would you accept tolerance? Or submission?

JEFF: Certainly not understanding. You can't understand why. Jenny can't understand why. She can't see that what the Colonel did, and what I want to do is for her. I would die for her.

JOHN: Has she asked you to? Sure, I have heard her say she wished you would. But, don't try to sell her that idea. You'd be surprised. Do you have any idea why she doesn't want her brother in the military? When she sees pictures of Vietnam, every mangled body that she sees is you. They are her brother, in another place, in another time, for another reason. But, they are all you. Every bloody casualty is you.

JEFF: I owe this to her. I owe this to you.

JOHN: How did you get this calling? When students in China are quoting Jefferson and Lincoln, and standing in front of tanks? When Solidarity has just replaced Communism in Poland? When Russia has just admitted that they were wrong to have invaded and occupied Afghanistan? And at this point in history you want to pick up a gun and go blow somebody away?

I don't think I heard Jenny begging you to do this for her. If you insist on a career in the military, you have to do that for yourself, not me, not Jenny. No thank you.

JEFF: There is no way we can talk about anything. I understand now how the Colonel felt. You have no pride or principle. You're a wimp. You think George Bush is a wimp! When you open the dictionary for a definition of wimp, you see a picture of John Bruner!

You and I both know that all this talk coming from the Communists is crap. Communism hasn't changed, at all. All those little countries aren't free yet. They won't let it happen. Maybe you'd be happy as a Communist?

JOHN: Would they let me keep the newspaper?

JEFF: You're funny!

JOHN: Would they let me go to church?

JEFF: No!

JOHN: Would they make me go to church?

JEFF: Of course they would! I mean, no they wouldn't. They would control your life. Communism is a dictatorship!

JOHN: Would they let me pray?

JEFF: I know where this conversation is going and I don't want to hear your same old liberal bullshit!

JOHN: Would they let me be a liberal?

JEFF: We are all going to be dead. There won't be any Liberals or Conservatives or anything. Nothing but Communists.

JOHN: I don't think I would like that. Do you mean we wouldn't have any televangelists, and skin-heads, and

pro-lifers, and Klansmen, and no National Rifle
Association, and no Republicans?

JEFF: They'd all be killed in the first week.

JOHN: Then they'd kill all the intellectuals, the liberals,
the gays, the humanists, and abortionists in the
second week?

JEFF: Forget it! Let me show you some logic that you can
understand. You see this Knight? *(Jeff picks up
John's Knight).* Let's take him away. Let's take away
this Stealth Bomber. *(Removing pieces one at a time
and placing them in his left hand)* Let's close a nuclear
plant. Let's take away a ballistic missle, and a few
tanks, and a battleship, an aircraft carrier, a rocket
launcher, and a regiment here and a battalion there.
(Leaving only a row of eight pawns on John's side) The
war is over!

JOHN: *(Looking at pawns)* What do I do now?

JEFF: In chess terms the word is "resign." In real life, the
time to do something has long passed. It's too late. If
you didn't do anything before, why would you want to
do something now?

Before I go to bed. Before we end this idiotic
discussion. Imagine this scene. A Russian soldier
knocks down your door, bursts into your office, sticks
a rifle in your face. What are your choices of
weapons?

JOHN: I don't know. You know more about guns than I
do.

JEFF: Pick up your weapon. Hit him with a rolled up
editorial. A typewriter is mightier than a sword. Hit
him with your typewriter. Reach into your pacifist

arsenal and defend yourself. Draw from your language skills and beg for your life. What do you think? That maybe he'll just go away?

JOHN: Jeff, don't do this! You've made your point!

JEFF: Don't beg to me. I'm not here anymore. You're talking to an armed Russian soldier. *(Pointing to a row of pawns)* What do we have left now? We have some English professors, some philosophers, some pacifists, some homosexuals, some paraplegics, some women, and some children. And what's this? *(Picking up one Pawn and handing it to John)* We have this one wimp, liberal, small town newspaper editor who never liked the marines. *(John looks at the Pawn in his hand)* Who never liked ROTC? Sorry about that, Mr. Bruner! There are no marines left! The war is over. You lost.

(Jeff points his right index finger at the Pawn in John's hand, makes a vocal sound to simulate a gun-shot, then blows imaginary smoke from the end of his finger, turns sharply and exits.)

(John looks at the Pawn in his hand, fondles it, folds his hands around it in a double fist, presses it to his forehead and bows his head.

Curtain

ACT III

Scene I

(Spring 1996)
Jennifer Bruner, college student
Resa, College Student
Margaret, College Student
Tracie, College Student
Lynne, College Student
Maria, College Student
Ginger, College Student
Carolyn, College Student
Kevin, College Student
Stuart, College Student
Alex, College Student
John Bruner, age 47
Mrs. John (Ellen) Bruner
Jeff Bruner, age 23

It is spring of 1996. Jenny Bruner is a member of a committee organizing an anti-war rally for the following day. It is part of a nationwide student demonstration to protest the presence of American Marines in El Salvador, sent for peace-keeping purposes following an outbreak of violence in that country.

The students are in Jenny's dorm room. Jenny is standing at a table thumbing through a stack of posters. The others are sitting on the floor around the room. Jenny holds up a poster that says, "Freedom For San Salvador."

JENNY: Okay, who did this poster?

ALL: *(At random)* Not me!

JENNY: I didn't think so. I want to be sure you all understand this. San Salvador is a city. El Salvador is a
country. San Salvador is the capital of El Salvador.
San Salvador is where the marines go to drink and do
whatever marines do. But, that's their problem, not
ours. What we are saying is that we should not have
sent troops to El Salvador. You do know where El
Salvador is, don't you?

MARGARET: It's in Central America.

GINGER: It's between Iowa and Kansas.

MARIA: You've been reading too much Dan Quayle!

GINGER: And they grow a lot of corn there.

JENNY: So, if Bush had sent you all instead of the
marines, we wouldn't have the problem, because you
never would have found the place. Are you ready to
do some serious planning for tomorrow?

MARIA: *(With dialect)* Lead on Senora Bruner! We will
follow you until our blood paints the countryside and
over- flows the rivers of our motherland!

JENNY: Over and over again. One message. Very
simple. It was a mistake to send American troops,
advisors or whatever they're called. This is a matter
to be settled by the Salvadorans. We can't keep on
trying to suppport right wing dictators in Central
America. Our goal for tomorrow is a minimum of two
thousand students. We may not get much media
coverage. Since this thing is nationwide, we surely
won't get any major network coverage. I'm sure at

least one Nashville camera crew will be here.
Anyway, we do need numbers. Just to make a
statement. We just really need a body count. We just
need warm bodies.

GINGER: Carolyn will represent Kappa Sig. She's their
warmest body.

JENNY: The messages on the signs are very important.
We may get two or three minutes on TV, and maybe
one short article, buried in the back of the newspaper.
But somebody may ask you some questions, and you
might be quoted. So, don't look dumb, or sound
dumb. At least sound like you know what you're
talking about.

TRACIE: I count eleven people here. Do you think the
crowd will turn out?

JENNY: Everything is perfectly co-ordinated. Trust me.
All the planning has been done. Everything will be in
place. The sound system is already hooked up. The
music department is setting up on the front steps of
the Student Union Building. We will have loud
speakers in most of trees around the English building
and in front of the library. We have lined up two
local folk groups...

RESA: Folk groups! Get out of the sixties, Jenny! Get
some funky stuff.

JENNY: We've got that! We've got three rock groups and
the two folk groups. We can use the funky stuff to
create some excitement. But, we've got to make a
statement. This is not a pep rally! Rock music draws
a crowd. After the speeches, we put on the folk
singers to make a statement. A peace message. With
some meaningful, lyrical, poetic protest songs.

RESA: Where've you been girl? That's your message. Not mine.

JENNY: Okay, just for you, we'll have them do a few verses of "We Shall Overcome." Or, are you strictly into rap lyrics? Maybe somebody could do a rap version of "We Shall Overcome".

RESA: You said lyrical poetry. I go either way, yours or mine.

JENNY: Haven't any of you read or heard anything about the sixties? The peace movement? The demonstrations? The freedom marches? The sit-ins?

ALEX: Jenny, I was born in seventy-five. I started to kindergarten the year Ronald Reagan was elected President. If you'll look at your American History book you'll find about four chapters that you haven't read yet. It's time you came out of the sixties, and looked around.

KEVIN: In a way Jenny's right. Between nineteen-seventy and nineteen-ninety, that history book is nothing but blank plain white empty pages. Nothing happened. Twenty years! Ford, Carter, Reagan, and Bush! What the hell can you write? Four pages maybe.

LYNNE: Jenny, I don't take issue with you on El Salvador. I'm with you all the way. But there are bigger things to deal with. The planet Earth is going to look like an open faced plastic sandwich on toast, with crude oil dressing, wrapped in disposable diapers. That's got to be priority one!

JENNY: The sixties and the nineties are both just moments in history. But the nineties belong to us. It's ours. We can't relive the sixties, or the age of the Greek philosophers, or the Renaissance/Reformation period, or the abolition of slavery, or women's suffrage, or the labor movement, or civil rights, or the anti-war movement. This is our only moment in history.

STUART: Open your eyes, Jenny. You're trying to be Bo Peep to sixteen thousand students who can't even spell the word Renaissance. They just want to get their degree and get a job. Leave them alone. Don't mess with their dreams. This is not their fight, it's yours.

LYNNE: Who knows? Tomorrow may be another Woodstock.

JENNY: I'm afraid there won't ever be another Woodstock. Things are never going to get bad enough for anything like that to ever happen again.

CAROLYN: We could all pull off our clothes and slide in the mud like they did, if it rains.

GINGER: When have you ever needed rain for a reason to pull your clothes off?

KEVIN: Jenny, the big problem is that you're treating this like an anti-war rally. This thing is not a war. The idea of war has no meaning to the American people since the wall came down. We do two things. We do peace-keeping, which they're calling this, and we do surgical strikes, like we did in Granada, Panama, Libya, and Colombia. We don't do wars anymore!

JENNY: We killed six thousand in Panama, and four thousand in Colombia. You don't call that war?

KEVIN: No, they don't last long enough. It takes at least four years to fight a war. We don't have the patience. You have to be an undeveloped country to fight a war

now. We were in Colombia three weeks. Most
people thought it was just another drug bust.

STUART: You know what I really miss about the
Communists? You don't know who anybody is
anymore! There is no "us" and "them" anymore!
When something you didn't like happened, you could
blame it on the Communists. How in the hell can we
fight wars without the Communists. There's a good
chance that your dinky-assed peace rally may last
longer than the Marines stay in El Salvador.

JENNY: There is a revolution going on in El Salvador!
Those people are fighting for freedom!

KEVIN: Freedom? Not freedom. They're just shooting
each other and whoever survives gets to pick the new
tyrant. It's their political process. Why should we
screw around with it?

ALEX: Why can't we just send them medicine, food, and
hand grenades and not get involved?

KEVIN: By definition, we really should consider it a civil
war. It's not a revolution. You have the rich land
owners on one side, and the peasants on the other
side. It's a civil war!

LYNNE: When the fighting is between the military and
the civilians it's a revolution. When you have two
armies then you can have a civil war.

ALEX: Don't put Civil War on any of the signs.
Somebody will see that on TV, and say, "I don't
remember no battle of Salvador. That must have
been up North somewhere. We need to go see that
next summer."

(Jenny holds up another sign. "Raiders 42, Eagles 7")

JENNY: Alex, has nothing meaningful happened in your world since the football season?

ALEX: Hey, it was a bowl game! We hadn't beaten Tech in four years!

CAROLYN: He had one date back in November, but I think that was before the last game.

MARIA: She said "meaningful." I know who he had a date with and I don't think you could consider little miss fluff princess "meaningful" if you were engaged to her!

STUART: Alex, did you know they have found that stupidity can be sexually transmitted?

KEVIN: The only thing she ever tested negative in was her ACT!

JENNY: Guys, that's enough bitch-bashing! Back to the subject of war, if it's not too boring.

JENNY: *(Picking up another poster)* Okay, who did the coat hanger? *(Holding up a drawing of a coat hanger)*

LYNNE: I did, but it's not finished. I was working on another project last night.

JENNY: Save it or trash it, but get it outta here. We're all with you on that, but not tomorrow. Tomorrow we just concentrate on El Salvador.

MARGARET: Point of order, Madam Chairladyperson. I beg to differ. I'm here because I feel for human life.

Human life is a very precious thing to me. I'm anti-war. I'm anti-military. I'm against capital punishment. I'm also very much against abortion. If this is an abortion rally, then I'm outta here!

JENNY: Margaret, ease up! This is just about El Salvador. Forget all the other stuff for right now.

MARGARET: The marines and the abortion clinics are both baby killers to me. Tomorrow, if the subject is El Salvador, we're on the same side. Then Tuesday we choose up sides again and go our separate ways.

GINGER: Did she say "choose?" The verb form of "choice?" Oops! Did Margaret, our little Southern Baptist maiden, utter a forbidden word?

LYNNE: Don't pay her any attention, Margaret. We don't tell you what to do with your life. You have the right to choose. We all believe in the right of choice.

MARGARET: I'm not stupid. I don't need an interpreter, Lynne. Besides, I'm not a Southern Baptist!

GINGER: What? Did you move?

RESA: They found out she's an abolitionist!

STUART: Margaret, you haven't gone soft on slavery! No! How could you? Don't you care about our traditions?

JENNY: Listen, everybody! Meet here at the room about nine-thirty. Pick up the signs and be ready to go and stay until its over. This is important. At exactly ten o'clock, everybody rushes out of the dorms, and we raise some hell.

TRACIE: But, I have a class at ten!

CAROLYN: Get real, Tracie! There are no classes
tomorrow.

TRACIE: Doctor Ramashani is not sympathetic to our
cause. He says that anyone who misses class
tomorrow is absent.

CAROLYN: Wow! The man is brilliant! If we had our
doctorates we could have figured that out.

JENNY: Tracie, we aren't studying history tomorrow,
we're making history.

TRACIE: It's not history, it's Introduction to Financial
Management. My daddy's giving me eight thousand
dollars a year for tuition. He says that every time I
miss a class, I waste forty-seven dollars of his money.

CAROLYN: See, you don't need to go to that class. You
can learn financial management from your old man.
He's a pro.

TRACIE: I've got to get my degree. He's gonna let me
run the business when I get out of school.

LYNNE: No way! The man's gonna live to be a hundred
and leave the store to your kid brother. The store
comes with the circumcision and the Bar Mizvah.
Drop out of school, take the man's tuition money and
buy Bloomingdale's from the Arabs or the Japanese,
or whoever. To hell with him and his forty-seven
dollars.

JENNY: Dammit, you are a pitiful bunch of
revolutionaries. You don't see anything serious about
this at all.

LYNNE: What! Of course we do! These things are
serious. We can't leave these great issues to be

determined by some ecclesiastics with divine calling, or some elected public officials. These questions need to be answered by those of us whose embryonic minds are being shaped into perfection on the academic assembly line of an institution of higher learning.

JENNY: I need to go over some minor details. We are working very closely with the campus police. They will have extra men on duty all day to control the crowd. We have also met with the city police. They will have squad cars ready to go if anything happens. Just in case it gets out of hand. What if Maria decides to torch the library?

MARIA: No way! Where do you think I get all my revolutionary ideas? But, that's a thought. What if we torch the ROTC building? No great ideas have ever come out of that place. It contributes nothing to the academic excellence of this campus.

GINGER: No! If the animals are asleep, don't rattle the cages.

KEVIN: Would you like to withdraw the last remark?

GINGER: Kevin, I'm sorry. You're just not the type. I forgot. I didn't mean it.

KEVIN: I agree with you. Not about the animal remark, but I do agree with you politically. I can be a political activist from ten to twelve, change uniforms, and go to ROTC from one to three. I can deal with that. I'm in the program because my family didn't have the tuition money. Uncle Sam is giving me four years of college and I'm giving him three years of my life for an education. And Margaret, that doesn't include killing any babies, for Uncle Sam or anybody else.

JENNY: Kevin, we love you. We know who you are, and
what you feel. We just didn't expect a lot of support
from the military science department. We've got the
English majors, the fine arts, and education
department. We just didn't expect you or the
marketing and finance department, or the aggies or
the jocks.

GINGER: Jenny, if we're cutting classes, we've got all the
jocks. It doesn't matter whether it's El Salvador or
Ground Hog Day.

JENNY: I know you all understand this, but I don't think
you really are excited about what's happening in the
world. In the last few years the world has changed so
much. Democracy and human rights have made more
progress around the world than ever before. It may
even catch on in America. One of these days, you'll
see somebody walking around quoting Jefferson or
Lincoln or the Declaration of Independence on the
streets of America. It's really beginning to happen. I
want you to feel this! Get emotional about it! Get
excited! Make it happen!

We were all born one generation too late. We don't
know what our parents went through. Kent State,
Montgomery, Chicago, and Little Rock. Resa, you
for example. How would you feel if they told you that
you couldn't eat at the lunch counter at Woolworth's
because you were black?

RESA: Woolworth's! Who the hell eats at Woolworth's?

JENNY: Okay, MacDonald's. What if they told you they
wouldn't serve you at MacDonald's?

RESA: No way! When the day comes that they won't serve
black people at MacDonald's, those folks are gonna
be in some big time kind of chapter eleven
bankruptcy trouble!

JENNY: Karen, you joke about living in a ghetto. Honey, River Oaks is not a ghetto. You may have a heavy ethnic concentration, but it's not a ghetto. In your neighborhood there are one point two doctors per household. We aren't talking about inner-city slums, crack-houses, and big hungry rats.

And, Margaret, the closest thing to pain that you have ever known was a broken finger-nail.

El Salvador is not like Granada or Panama. This is something very different. El Salvador is Spanish for Vietnam! Surely, we must have learned something from Vietnam!

Jenny picks up another poster. "Exodus 20:13"

JENNY: Who's the Bible thumper?

STUART: I'm going after the rural fundamentalist vote. It's an appeal to divine authority. Infallibility! Inerrancy!

JENNY: But it doesn't mean anything to anybody. What does it say?

STUART: Sure it does. They all had to learn it in school when they were kids. They use it like bumper stickers and flash cards. You just toss out book, chapter, and verse. Nobody is going to question that. They all know what it says! You don't question it!

JENNY: We aren't all fundamentalists. You're going to have to tell us what it says.

STUART: It says "Thou shall not kill." We all learned to
    recite it. Then they told us stories about David and
    and Goliath and Samson bashing the Phillistines.
    You could kill Gentiles, but couldn't kill another Jew.
    But, the Klan explained to them that Jesus wasn't a
    Jew. So then they could kill anybody as long as they
    didn't go to the same church you did. The Old
    Testament is hard to understand if you're not a Bible
    scholar.

GINGER: Stuart, you surprise me. I didn't know you
    were a Bible scholar. Do you take that stuff seriously?

STUART: If you're going to be a scholar, you have to read
    everything. If something is true, it doesnt matter who
    wrote it or where you read it, it's still the truth.

GINGER: But, you're not religious. Margaret is the one
    who's religious. You can't be. Are you some kind of
    closet Christian that we don't know about?

STUART: It's different. Margaret's not going to get killed
    in El Salvador. Baptists don't get killed fighting for
    human rights. It's the Catholic priests who are being
    killed in El Salvador.

RESA: I don't recall Martin Luther King being an
    Archbishop. He died fighting for civil rights.

ALEX: What's the difference?

RESA: Color! If you're a black Baptist preacher it's civil
    rights. If you're a white Catholic priest, it called
    human rights. And it depends on whether you get
    killed in Memphis or El Salvador.

ALEX: What about white Baptist preachers?

JENNY: Catholic priests are being killed in El Salvador
with guns that we gave the Salvadoran government.
Does that not bother you at all. Don't you feel any
guilt at all.

ALEX: I know a preacher who got fired over the civil
rights thing. The man was making about forty
thousand a year and he lost his job.

GINGER: That doesn't count. You don't understand,
Alex. We're talking about martyrdom. Not
unemployment.

ALEX; He got a job. He's selling mutual funds or
something. He's just not preaching anymore.

*Jenny excitedly shows them another poster, carefully
lettered, that reads, "East Germany, Estonia, Lithuania,
El Salvador."*

JENNY: This may be the most effective statement I have
seen. This is what it's all about. That freedom from
oppression has to be universal, not just in Eastern
Europe. It's like enforcing the Monroe Doctrine on
ourselves.

STUART: The man who's been sitting watching sit-coms
for three hours is not going to understand that.

JENNY: Everybody watches the ten o'clock news.
Intellectuals will even close a book to watch the news.
Especially, the local news.

STUART: I'm serious. The sit-com addict with a two digit
IQ, is not going to make the connection on that.

JENNY: Stuart, some people you can teach, some you can inspire, others you just have to try to confuse as best you can. You do whatever works.

MARGARET: I know we all believe what we're doing tomorrow is the the right thing to do. But, what if something goes wrong. What if they call out the National Guard? Or if it turns into a riot and we all get put in jail?

JENNY: That was back in the sixties. That can't happen now. Another thing, and this is just one more precaution. When you pick up your signs tomorrow, don't fasten them to sticks. Every time there's been a peace rally, some fool hits somebody across the face with a stick. Then some photographer takes a picture of a bloody nose and it looks like we had a riot. It's just another part of the non-violent thing. We can't let anything go wrong.

GINGER: And besides, you might poke your eye out with a stick. That's what my grandma always used to tell me.

JENNY: Remember who you are, and what the peace rally is all about. If you paint any signs or posters, don't do anything that looks like an anti-American message. We aren't going to burn any flags, and we aren't going to wave any flags. We aren't taking sides on this. It doesn't matter whether it's a Salvadoran soldier, or an American soldier, they're all still some mother's child. We just need to make them stop killing each other!

We'll meet back here tomorrow night to watch the six o'clock news to see if anybody heard us.

Wait. Don't leave yet. Remember, tomorrow is not prom night, or Greek week, or a keg party. We did tell some of the guys over at the frat houses that it was so they would show up.

Before you go. I need for you to listen for just a minute. I need to practice my speech. It's not long. I promise. Please!

In the last fifteen years, ninety-thousand Salvadorans have been murdered. They were farmers, peasants, women, children, nuns and priests. They were killed by guns made in America and given to the government of El Salvador, by the government of the United States. I don't want you to go to bed tonight without some feeling of shame for what we have done. I want you to lay awake and think about it for a little while.

I want you to see in your mind the battered faces, the bloody bodies lying on the street by the curb. I want you to see the dirty children scrounging through the garbage heaps looking for food. I want you to see the the cardboard and tin shacks that the Salvadorans live in. Ninety thousand of these people were murdered by the Salvadoran military with our blessing.

Now other people are being killed. The journalists, the diplomatic staff, the generals, the colonels, the land-owners, the government officials. The rebels now have our automatic rifles. This we call terrorism. Now we're concerned. We waited too long, did the wrong thing, with the wrong weapons, to the wrong people, for all the wrong reasons.

We didn't care when the farmers and the peasants were killed. But, next week when we lose our first marine, when the first peace-keeper is killed by sniper fire, everybody will care. You aren't going to get concerned until somebody you know gets killed. Some kid that you went to high school with. Then it becomes a tragedy. Then it becomes real. In spite of all we do tomorrow, the Salvadoran military and the rebels will both still be shooting the farmers, the peasants, the children, the women, the priests, the nuns, and the journalists.

We don't need more guns and more tanks and more bombs in El Salvador. We don't need to be fighting this war. You can't stop a revolution with guns. The British learned it from Patrick Henry and from Ghandi. The French learned it from the Vietnamese. The Russians learned it from the East Germans, the Latvians, the Estonians, and the Lithuanians. Maybe tomorrow we can help America learn from the Salvadorans. That's what tomorrow is all about.

Thanks! Just in case I screw it up tomorrow, then you know what I was trying to say. Thank you all for listening.

(The students sit motionless, in deep thought, exchange meaningful glances, without getting up to leave.)

Curtain

Scene II

The scene opens in the den of the Bruner home. It is the following afternoon (Tuesday). Mrs. Bruner is putting medication and a bandage on the palm of Jenny's right hand. Jenny and her mother have been crying and are trying to comfort each other.

(John Bruner enters right.)

JOHN: *(He rushes to Jenny and looks at her hand.)* What happened? Why are you home? I saw your car in the driveway. Are you hurt?

JENNY: It's just a few scratches. It's okay. Sit down and I'll try to tell you everything that I remember. Everything's okay. It's just a long story and I'm not thinking very straight. We had the demonstration today. You know. I told you we were planning it...

JOHN: I know. I sent a reporter, but she hadn't come back when I left the office. What happened?

JENNY: I don't know where to begin. *(Jenny's story is broken and with long pauses, sobs, and attempts to regain her composure.)*

The demonstration began on schedule, around ten. We had half the student body. Maybe more than that. It was so much bigger than we had expected...

The whole area between the library and the Student Union Building was covered with people...

We started with the music. The bands were great.
We had some good groups. The students were
singing along and dancing. After a while, we stopped
the music, and started to introduce the speakers. The
students yelled for the musicians to start playing
again...

We had painted some signs. By that that time the
signs were all laying on the ground and everybody was
dancing on them...

Everybody was chanting and yelling...

I had written a good speech and I never got to make
it. Nobody made a speech...

It was nothing but a rock concert. Nobody cared
about El Salvador. You couldn't tell that anybody
knew what it was all about...

JOHN: Jenny, I'm sorry. I was afraid that would happen.
You expected too much.

JENNY: A lot of the guys brought kegs, and turned it into
a tail-gate party. A lot of them were already drunk at
ten o'clock...

Some girl in a yellow neon tank-top started dancing
on one of the benches over at the library and all the
guys crowded over there to watch her...

Kevin and I came down off the steps, and were
talking about going back to the dorm...

All the planning we had put in it...

We just lost it...

I can't believe it happened...

We were standing there at the corner of the building looking at some flowers. I started crying...

I reached down and picked a rose. One that was just about to open. A yellow one. I just have a thing about yellow roses. I stuck a thorn in my finger. I was squeezing the stem between my thumb and finger to stop the bleeding...

JOHN: You scared me. I thought you had really gotten hurt.

JENNY: I held the stem between my finger and thumb to avoid the thorns and to stop the bleeding...

While I was looking at the rose, everything got very quiet. I climbed the steps so I could see. Down toward East Main, there was a convoy of army trucks turning onto campus and coming around the circle...

The students would move back to let the trucks pass, and then follow behind, yelling and waving their arms at the soldiers on the trucks...

They would beat on the sides of the trucks and make gestures at the soldiers...

There were maybe ten or twelve trucks. They formed a semi-circle, and the soldiers got out and formed lines between the trucks and the students...

I was still standing on the steps, watching. We had talked about this, even laughed about it, but we never really thought something like this would ever happen...

The soldiers had on riot gear. Helmets, gas masks.
Their rifles were slung over their shoulders. No
bayonets. The officers had pistols in holsters. Most
of them had those shield-like looking things and long
riot sticks...

Some of our guys teased them. They took off their
shirts and waved them at the soldiers, and then ran. It
was like somebody trying to intimidate a bull. To
make it chase them or maybe drive it away. It was
such a farce. It was as if it was all a joke. The
students tried to be macho, and then they would run...

They would get close to the soldiers, wave their
hands, or wave their shirts and then jump back. A lot
of the students went back into the dorms and watched
from their windows. Most of the girls had left...

I don't know why I did what I did. I was either brave
or stupid, I don't know. I was still crying. I just
walked through the crowd. Toward the soldiers. I
wasn't scared. I don't even know if I knew where I
was going. It seems like a dream...

The soldiers looked like monstors. Their gas masks
were so ugly. They didn't look human. They looked
like something out of a science fiction movie. They
had no faces. They were so awful looking. I guess I
didn't have enough sense to be afraid...

For some reason, at that point, I realized. This is real.
This is what we had planned. We were out here to
make a statement and I had completely forgotten...

This was not a rock concert any more...

And when I realized that, I was scared...

But, I still did this stupid thing...

I walked toward one of them. I chose one that didn't have a riot stick or rifle. He just had a pistol on his belt. I knew he was an officer. I stood about six feet away and I offered him the rose I had picked.

I held it up and reached out to him with it. I said something dumb like "Flowers are better than bullets." I'm not sure what I said. He was so terrifying with the gas mask on...

He moved his right hand ...

I didn't know if he was going to take the rose or take out his pistol and shoot me...

He raised his gas mask, and he looked at me, and he said, "My God, Jenny, how did we ever come to this?"...

JOHN: Jeff!

JENNY: I turned and ran to the dorm. I didn't look back. I went to my room and fell on my bed and buried my face, and cried. Then, I felt this horrible pain, and looked at my hand, and I had been squeezing the stem of the rose. The flower was broken off, and I had been squeezing the thorns...

Blood was running off my fingers on the bedspread...

I lay there crying for a while. I don't know how long. Then I heard a lot of yelling and the trucks started up and were pulling away. The students were yelling. There was a lot of confusion. The soldiers were yelling, and running in different directions. The students were running along side the trucks...

I couldn't tell who anybody was. I couldn't see Jeff. He must have been on one of the trucks. One officer

in a jeep was blowing his horn and yelling. I don't
know if somebody got hurt. I didn't hear any shots. I
just jumped in my car and came home...

Mom and I tried to call Jeff twice. The first time they
said he had not come back yet. The second time they
said he had left and they were looking for him...

How could I have known it would be Jeff? What if
he's in some kind of trouble? What if somebody got
hurt? Why would the soldiers just leave like that?

JOHN: Calm down. Rest a minute. It's okay. Jeff is okay.
We would have heard from him if anything had
happened. He'll call us tonight. There's nothing to
worry about. He'll call.

JENNY: Can we drive up to Fort Campbell and see him? I
can't believe I did something so stupid. I just feel like
something must be wrong. Why would they be
looking for him? Why didn't I stay and talk to him?
Why did I have to run away?

ELLEN: Let me stay here in case he calls. You two drive
up and check on him, and call me when you find out
something. I'm sure he's okay. Do I need to change
your bandage and put some medicine on your hand?

JENNY: It doesn't hurt anymore. Dad, why don't you
drive? I don't have any gas in my car. I almost didn't
make it home. I got blood all over the steering wheel.

*(The door opens. Jeff enters right. Jenny runs to him, hugs
him, presses the side of her face to his chest, facing front
stage, not looking at him.)*

JENNY: Jeff, I'm sorry! I didn't mean for this to happen.

JEFF: *(Holding her bandaged hand and looking down at her)* What happened? How did you do this?

JENNY: Why did the trucks leave? When I looked out the window, they were all leaving. Is anything wrong? Jeff, I'm sorry I did that. I didn't know it would be you.

(With their arms around each other they walk to center stage and sit across from each other, leaning forward and touching hands)

JEFF: I saw you on the steps when I got off the truck. I knew you would be in the middle of everything. I even asked not to be on this assignment. This was my first job as executive officer. My first assignment as a first lieutenent, and I really had no choice.

JENNY: Jeff, I'm really sorry. I didn't mean to cause you any trouble.

JEFF: While I was driving home, I kept thinking about all the fights we've had. You and I have been fighting ever since we were old enough to think. I kept thinking about the day I left to go to basic training. The whole trip to the airport, you kept telling me how crazy I was to have enlisted. Then at the airport, you hugged me and told me you loved me. I knew that, but it was nice to hear.

Today, I looked for you. Then I saw you go up the steps. I wanted to talk to you, and hug you and I couldn't do that.

I wanted to hold you and tell you I loved you, but you
ran away...

I just froze. I stood there not knowing what to do...

I don't know why we were there. We didn't think we
were coming. We were on stand-by and ready to
move...

Then the city police called and said they couldn't
handle the crowd and wanted us to back them up...

It may have been the Captain's idea. It was the first
chance he had to see if all the training works...

Tears were running down my face inside the mask
and I couldn't see...

That never happened in any of the drills...

Jenny, I stood there thinking about the arguments
and the fights you and I have had...

Today was different. I was armed with a forty-five
and you came at me armed with a rose. I hadn't been
trained for that kind of confrontation...

It wasn't fair...

When you started to run, I heard this sound behind
me. I know I heard it. I have heard that sound so
many times. It was the click of someone loading a
clip into a rifle. We didn't bring any ammunition, live
or blank. I don't know how he got it. But, I know I
heard it...

I watched you run. I watched you until you went
inside the dorm...

I closed my eyes, I guess. But I kept seeing a picture
that you have on your wall at home. The Kent State
picture that I have just looked at and never thought
much about...

I could see you lying on the ground. With blood all
all over you. And I could see Ginger looking up at
me and screaming. She was on her knees, with her
hands in the air...

She was looking up at me and screaming and calling
me a murderer...

I turned around and gave the order to get on the
trucks. I didn't have that authority. I was second in
command...

By the time the Captain got to us, most of the trucks
were pulling out onto East Main. He followed
behind until we reached the interstate, then pulled us
over...

He chewed me out standing on the side of the
interstate. He told me to report to his office after the
equipment was secured and the troops dismissed...

I had everybody searched for ammunition, but we
didn't find any. Maybe I didn't hear it. I don't know.
I thought I did...

By the time I got to the Captain's office, he and the
Sargeant had discussed the matter at length and
called the Regimental Commander. I have to report
in the morning at eight for a preliminary hearing...

JENNY: What will they do to you? You didn't do anything
wrong. Jeff, I'm sorry. It's all my fault.

JEFF: More than likely just a reduction in grade back to
second lieutenant. And relieved of duty as executive
officer. I hope they will transfer me to another unit.
The Captain is pretty bent out of shape about this. I
don't think I could ever work with him anymore...

The regimental commander has a daughter in college.
That's gotta be to my advantage. I think he might
understand. I just need to talk to him when the
captain is not around...

The worst they would do would be some period of
confinement to quarters. Not in the stockade. Just
maybe confined to the barracks...

It would be funny if they did send me to the stockade.
That out of this family of radicals and revolutionaries,
that I would be the only one to go to jail for a crime of
conscience...

JENNY: Don't joke about that. It's not funny. You're a
good soldier. They couldn't put you in prison for this.
You did what was right. Somebody might have gotten
hurt today.

JEFF: I wonder what the Colonel would have done today.
I don't think he would have been very proud of me.

JOHN: He would have done exactly what you did. He was
a much better man that I ever gave him credit for
being. Most of what you are came from him. The
Colonel never had to face a sister armed with a rose.
He would be proud of you.

JEFF: The official charge is "insubordination". It will go
on my record. I may be a second lieutenent forever.
They have to do something. The least would be a
verbal reprimand, but the Captain has already done a
pretty super job on that already...

Anyway, the hearing is at eight o'clock. It would be
good if you'all could come up and meet me for lunch
when it's over. I'll be at the headquarters building,
second regiment. It's the big brick building across
from the parade field. It's where we had graduation
when I finished OCS. You saw it when you came up
to see me then. I'll meet you on the front steps as
soon as the hearing is over.

JENNY: We could drive up tonight and stay over and
meet you for breakfast. I would feel so much better.
I did this to you. Let me go with you and tell them.

JEFF: I appreciate that, but they go by a different book. It
says that captains out-rank first lieutenents. That's
the bottom line. There is nothing in the Uniform
Code of Military Justice about legal representation by
your sister. The fact that you love me, doesn't have
much impact on the Captain. He's too professional
for any kind of human emotions. He has no family.
Just the Army. That's all he knows. He'd like a court
martial. What he saw was a riot. This was what he'd
been trained for, and I messed it up for him...

But you're safe. Jenny, I love you. I do feel good
about what I did. I would do the same thing again
even if I had time to think about it...

I've gotta go. They may still be looking for me and I
will wind up in the stockade...

*(Jeff gets up to leave. Jenny gets up, reaching for him. He
backs away, with Jenny holding his arm. He backs into a
table with a chess board on it. The chess pieces fall to the
floor. He catches the table and board and keeps them
from turning over and returns them to an upright position,
near front center stage, and walks backward toward the
exit to foyer at right.)*

ELLEN: Hurry, Jeff! I'll pick that up. Just go. Be careful, but hurry!

(Jeff, John, and Jenny exit to foyer)

(Mrs. Bruner kneels to floor behind the table and picks up three pawns, one at a time and randomly places them on the chess board. Without picking up the others, she rushes to the foyer to join the others off-stage)

JOHN: *(Offstage)* We'll be there a little after eight in case you get out early. Call us tonight when you get there. We love you, Son!

JENNY: Be careful, Jeff! I love you.

JEFF: Good night! I love you all!

(Dim lights, except front center for focus on chess board with the three pawns)

Curtain